The Fisherman a

by Oscar Wi

CHAPTER ONE

The Mermaid

Every evening the fisherman went out fishing. He sometimes sold his fish at the market. Sometimes he did not catch many fish and he could not sell them.

One evening his net was very heavy. He laughed and said, 'Did I catch all the fish in the sea? Or did I catch some horrible monster? I will give it to the Queen. She will be happy.'

He pulled and pulled the heavy net. Finally, he pulled the net next to the boat.

But there were no fish in it and there was no monster. There was only a little mermaid. She was asleep.

Her hair was yellow like gold; her body was white like ivory; her tail like silver and pearl; and her ears like seashells.

She was very beautiful. The fisherman pulled the net closer to the boat. He embraced her. When he touched her, she screamed.

She could not escape so she began to cry and said, 'Please let me go. I am the only daughter of a King of the Sea. My father is very old and alone.'

But the fisherman answered her, 'I will let you go, but you must make me a promise. I will call you and you will come and sing to me. The fish love the songs of the people of the sea. You will sing and my nets will be full.'

'I promise. Please let me go,' cried the mermaid.

'Yes, I will let you go,' said the fisherman. So she promised him and he let her go. She went back into the sea and trembled. She felt a strange fear.

Every evening the young fisherman went fishing and called the mermaid. She came and sang to him. The dolphins swam round and round her. The seagulls were in the sky above her head.

She sang a marvellous song of the tritons, the men with long green beards.

She sang of the gardens of the sea with their corals. Here the fish swim like silver birds.

She sang of the big whales from the cold north seas, and of the dead sailors in their ships at the bottom of the sea.

She sang of the little children. They ride on the backs of the dolphins and laugh.

When she sang the tuna fish came to listen to her. The young fisherman then caught many of them.

When his boat was full of fish, the mermaid smiled at him and swam away.

But she never came near him. When he tried to catch her, she went into the water like a seal. Each day her voice became sweeter to his ears. Soon he forgot his nets and listened to her song. He listened to her until the moon came.

One evening he called her, and said, 'Little mermaid, marry me because I love you.'

But the little mermaid said, 'You have a human soul. Send away your soul, and then I can love you.'

The young fisherman thought, 'Why do I need my soul? I cannot see it. I cannot touch it. I do not know it. Of course I will send it away and I will be very happy.'

He stood up in his boat and cried, 'I will send my soul away! You will be my wife, and you will show me all the things you sing about. We will be together forever.'

The little mermaid laughed because she was very happy.

'But how can I send my soul away?' cried the young fisherman. 'I do not know,' said the little mermaid. 'The people of the sea have no souls.'

Early the next morning the fisherman went to the priest's house and knocked on his door. The priest looked out of the window and saw the fisherman and said, 'Come in.'

The young fisherman entered and cried to the priest, 'Father, I am in love with a mermaid. I cannot marry her because I have a soul. How can I send my soul away? I really do not need it. Why is my soul important? I cannot see it. I cannot touch it. I do not know it.'

The priest answered, 'Are you mad? God gave you your soul. It is very precious. It is as precious as all the gold in the world. So, my son, do not think about this any more. It is the worst sin. The people of the sea are lost creatures. They are like the beasts of the fields. They do not know what is right and wrong. God didn't die for them.'

The young fisherman began to cry and said, 'Father, the fauns live in the forest and are happy. The mermen sit on the rocks with their gold harps. I want to be like them.

'Why is my soul important? I have a soul, but I cannot have the mermaid, and I love her,' he cried.

'It is horrible to love your body!' cried the priest. 'The fauns of the woods and the mermen are horrible! I hear them at night. They try to distract me from my prayers. They are lost, I tell you, they are lost. There is no heaven or hell for them.'

'Away! Away!' cried the priest. 'Your mermaid is lost and you will be lost with her.'

The young fisherman walked sadly to the marketplace.

When the merchants saw him they said, 'What do you want to sell?'

'I will sell you my soul,' he answered. 'Please buy it from me because I am tired of it. What can I do with a soul? I cannot see it. I cannot touch it. I do not know it.'

But the merchants laughed at him, and said, 'What can we do with a soul? A false coin is more precious. Sell us your body, and we will give you a lot of gold. But we will not give you any money for your soul.'

The young fisherman thought, 'How strange this is! The priest said, "Your soul is as precious as all the gold in the world." But the merchants say, "A false coin is more precious."'

He went to the beach and began to think.

CHAPTER TWO

The Witch

At midday he remembered that there was a young witch. She lived in a cave and she was very good at magic. He ran quickly to her.

'What do you need? What do you need?' she cried, when he ran towards her cave. 'Do you need fish when the weather is bad? I have a special instrument. You play it and all the fish swim into the bay. But it has a price, pretty boy, it has a price.

'What do you need? What do you need? A storm to destroy the ships? Do you want the gold on the ships? I can help you. I have more storms than the wind. My master is stronger than the wind. But I have a price, pretty boy, I have a price.'

'I do not want very much,' said the young fisherman, 'but the priest is very angry with me, and the merchants laugh at me. So, I came to you, and I will pay you any price.'

'What do you want?' asked the witch.

'I want to send my soul away from me,' answered the young fisherman.

The witch's face became white. 'Pretty boy, pretty boy,' she said, 'that is a terrible thing to do.'

He laughed and answered her, 'My soul is not important to me. I cannot see it. I cannot touch it. I do not know it.'

'I will tell you, but you must give me something,' said the witch. She looked at him with her beautiful eyes.

'Five pieces of gold,' he said, 'and my nets and my house, and my boat. But how can I send away my soul?'

She laughed and answered, 'I can change the autumn leaves into gold. I can change the light of the moon into silver. My master is richer than all the kings of this world.'

The witch caressed his hair with her thin white hand. 'You must dance with me, pretty boy,' she said softly, and she smiled at him.

'Only this?' cried the young fisherman.

'Only this,' she answered, and she smiled at him again.

'Then we will dance together in a secret place at sunset,' he said, 'and you will tell me everything. Then I can send away my soul.'

'When the moon is full, when the moon is full,' she said softly. Then she looked around and listened. Three birds sang. There was no other sound. There was only the sound of the waves. So she pulled him next to her. She put her dry lips close to his ear.

'Tonight you must come to the top of the mountain,' she whispered. 'It is a special night and He will be there.'

'Who is He?' he asked.

'It is not important,' she answered. 'Go tonight and stand under the tree, and wait for me. You will see a dog, and you must hit it with a stick. The dog will run away. Remember, do not speak to the owl. I will come with the full moon, and we will dance together.'

'How can I send my soul away? You must promise to tell me,' he said.

She came out of the cave into the sun. T promise,' she answered.

'You are the best witch in the world,' cried the fisherman, and he ran back to the town happily.

The witch went into her cave, and burned a magic plant. She looked into the smoke.

After some time she said angrily, 'He must be mine. I am as beautiful as she is.'

That evening, when the moon appeared, the fisherman went to the top of the mountain. He stood under the tree.

A big owl with yellow eyes called his name. He did not answer. A black dog ran towards him. He hit it with the stick, and it ran away.

At midnight the witches were in the sky. They were like bats. 'Phew!' they cried when they came to the ground, 'there is someone here and we do not know him!'

Finally, the young witch with red hair appeared. She wore a gold dress with peacock's eyes on it and her little hat was green.

'Where is he, where is he?' asked the witches when they saw her. She laughed and ran to the fisherman. She took him by the hand and then they danced in the moonlight.

They danced round and round. Then they heard the sound of a galloping horse, but they did not see a horse.

'Faster, faster!' she cried, and then the fisherman was afraid. Something very bad was there and he was afraid of it.

There was a man near a rock. He wore elegant Spanish clothes. This man watched the fisherman constantly. The witch laughed, and he danced with her round and round.

CHAPTER THREE

The Secret

A dog barked and the dancers stopped. They went to the man, and kissed his hand.

'Come! Let's pray,' the witch said softly. The fisherman wanted to do this, and he followed her. But when he came near the man, he called God's name.

When he did this, the witches screamed and went away. A horse came and the man got on it. He looked at the fisherman sadly, and then disappeared.

The witch with red hair tried to fly away too, but the fisherman stopped her.

'Let me go,' she cried. 'You must not say God's name.'

'No,' he answered, 'You are my prisoner. Tell me the secret now.'

'What secret?' said the witch. She tried to escape.

'You know,' he answered.

She began to cry and said to the fisherman, 'Ask me anything, but not that!'

He laughed, and didn't want to release her.

She could not escape and so she said, 'I am as beautiful as the mermaids,' and she put her face near his.

But he pushed her away and said, 'I will kill you. You must tell me the secret now.'

She trembled. 'All right,' she said. 'It is your soul, not mine.'

She gave him a little knife.

'Why did you give me this knife?' he asked.

She was silent for a moment. She was terrified. Then she said to him, 'Our shadow is not the shadow of our bodies. It is the body of our souls. Stand on the beach with your back to the moon. Cut your shadow from your feet. Then you must tell your soul to leave and it will leave.'

The young fisherman trembled. 'Is this true?' he said.

He released her and took the knife. Then he walked to the sea.

The fisherman's soul then said to him, 'I am your servant. Do not send me away now. Did I do anything bad to you?'

The young fisherman laughed. 'You didn't do anything bad, but I do not need you,' he answered.

'The world is big. Go where you want. But do not disturb me because my love is calling me.'

His soul called him many times, but he did not listen.

He then arrived on the beach and stood on the sand with his back to the moon. White arms came out of the foam and they asked him to come.

His soul said to him, 'Do not send me away without a heart. The world is cruel. Give me your heart.'

'How can I love my mermaid without a heart?' he cried.

'Please,' said his soul, 'give me your heart. The world is cruel and I am afraid.'

'My heart is with my love now,' he answered. 'Go away.'

'But I also need to love,' said his soul.

'Go away. I do not need you!' cried the young fisherman.

He took the little knife and cut his shadow from his feet. The shadow stood up in front of him, and it was very similar to the fisherman.

The fisherman moved back slowly, and he was afraid. 'Go away!' he murmured, 'and never come back again.'

'No, but we must meet again,' said the soul. The soul's voice was like a flute.

'How will we meet?' cried the young fisherman. 'Will you follow me into the sea?'

'Once every year I will come to this place, and call you,' said the soul. 'Perhaps you will need me.'

'I do not think I will need you,' cried the young fisherman, 'but you can call me. I can come here again.' He went into the water, and the tritons played their musical instruments. The little mermaid came to meet him. She put her arms around his neck and kissed him on the mouth.

The soul stood on the beach and watched them. And when they disappeared into the sea, the fisherman's soul walked away and cried.

CHAPTER FOUR

The Soul's First Journey

After a year, the soul came down to the sea and called the young fisherman. He came out of the sea, and said, 'Why do you call me?'

The soul answered, 'Come nearer. I want to speak to you because I saw marvellous things.'

So he came nearer, and sat in the water and listened.

The soul said to him, 'When I left you, I went towards the East and travelled. Everything wise comes from the East. After six days I came to the land of the Tartars. One night I saw a fire in a camp of a company of merchants. I went to them and the chief of merchants stood up and took his sword.

'"Who are you?" he asked.

'"I am a Prince and I escaped from the Tartars," I replied.

'He lowered his head as a sign of respect and took my hand.

'Then we left the country of the Tartars and we travelled in many strange lands and saw many strange people. I travelled on a camel next to the chief. There were forty camels in the caravan and eighty mules.

'During our journey we battled with the tribe of the Magadae. They are born old and grow younger every year, and die when they are little children. We battled with the Laktroi. They think they are the sons of tigers, and they paint their bodies yellow and black. We also battled with the Sibians. They have horses' feet and they run quicker than horses.

'In the fourth month we arrived in the city of Illel. It was night and we waited for day to come.

That morning we knocked at the gate of the city. The gate was of red bronze and it had images of sea-dragons and dragons with wings.

'A guard then said to us, "What do you want?"

'"We are from the island of Syria and we have a lot of merchandise to sell," we answered.

'"Then wait here until midday," he said.

'At midday they opened the gates and we went to the marketplace.

'After a month in the city of Illel, I became tired of it. I walked in the streets of the city and came to the garden of the god of the city.

The priests in their yellow tunics walked silently in the garden. There was a red house. This was the home of the god. The doors had images of golden animals and peacocks on them.

'There was a pool of clear water in front of the temple. I sat down near it. One of the priests came to me and stood behind me.

'"What do you want?" he asked me.

'"I want to see the god," I replied.

'"The god is hunting in a forest," said the priest, and he looked at me strangely.

'"Which forest is he in? Tell me, and I will go there," I answered.

'He moved his hands on his soft tunic. "The god is asleep," he murmured.

'"Which bed is he in? Tell me, and I will stand near him," I answered.

'"The god is at the feast," he cried.

'"I will drink bitter or sweet wine with him," I said.

'He was surprised and accompanied me into the temple.

'In the first room I saw an ebony idol on a throne and it the size of a man. There was a ruby on its forehead. Its feet were red from the blood of a baby goat.

'I said to the priest, "Is this the god?"

'"This is the god," he answered.

'"This is not the god. Show me the god," I cried, "or I will kill you." I touched his hand, and it became small and dry.

'"Make my hand better, and I will show you the god," he cried.

'So I breathed on his hand, and it became better. He trembled and accompanied me into the second room. I saw an ivory idol on a lotus of jade with great emeralds on it. This idol was twice as big as a man.

'"Is this the god?" I asked him.

'"This is the god," he replied.

'"This is not the god. Show me the god," I cried, "or I will kill you!" I touched his eyes, and they became blind.

'"Please make my eyes better. Then I will show you the god," he cried.

'So I breathed on his eyes and they could see again. The priest trembled and accompanied me into the third room. There was not an idol in it, only a mirror.

'I said to the priest, "Where is the god?"

'He answered me, "There is no god, but this is the Mirror of Wisdom. It reflects all the things in heaven and on earth. But it does not reflect the face of the person if they look into it. So, this person can become wise. There are many other mirrors, but they are mirrors of Opinion. This is the only Mirror of Wisdom. When you possess this mirror, you know everything. So, it is a god, and we pray to this god." I looked into the mirror. The priest didn't lie.

'Then I did something strange, but it is not important. I placed the mirror in a valley near here. We can walk there in three days. Let me enter you again and be your servant, and you will have wisdom.'

But the young fisherman laughed. 'Love is better than wisdom,' he cried, 'and the little mermaid loves me.'

'No, there is nothing better than wisdom,' said the soul.

'Love is better,' answered the young fisherman. He went back to the sea, and the soul walked away and cried.

CHAPTER FIVE

The Riny of Rihes

After the second year, the soul came down to the sea and called the young fisherman. He came out of the sea and said, 'Why do you call me?'

The soul answered, 'Come nearer. I want to speak to you because I saw marvellous things.'

So he came nearer, and sat in the water and listened.

The soul said to him, 'When I left you, I went towards the South and travelled. Everything precious comes from the South.

'I travelled six days to the city of Ashter. I saw the city on the morning of the seventh day.

'The city is like a bazaar. It is wonderful. Merchants sit on silk carpets. Some of them sell strange perfumes from the islands of the Indian Sea, and the oil of red roses. Other merchants sell fantastic jewellery with tiger claws in gold and leopard claws in gold also.

'The people sell all kinds of fruit: purple figs, yellow melons, white grapes, red-gold oranges and oval lemons of green gold. I saw an elephant. It stopped and began eating the oranges and the people laughed. You cannot imagine how strange these people are. When they are happy they buy a bird in a cage. Then they release the bird because they want to be happier. When they are sad they hit their bodies with thorns because they want to be sadder.

'On the feast of the New Moon, the Emperor came out of his palace and went into the mosque to pray. The people covered their faces, but I showed him no form of respect.

'That night the guards of the Emperor came for me. They accompanied me into the palace. We walked across a great court and then we entered a beautiful garden. At the end of the garden there was a pavilion. Then the captain of the guard told me to enter.

'The young Emperor was there on a bed of lion skins, and he held a falcon. A Nubian stood behind him. A large scimitar of steel was on a table next to the bed.

'When the Emperor saw me he was worried, and said to me, "What is your name? Don't you know that I am Emperor of this city?" I did not answer him.

'He indicated the scimitar, and the Nubian took it and hit me with great violence. It did not hurt me. The Nubian was terrified and went away.

'The Emperor tried to kill me with a lance but he didn't hurt me. He tried to kill me with an arrow, but I stopped it in the air. Then the Emperor said to me, "Why can't I hurt you? Are you a prophet or the son of a prophet? Please leave my city tonight. You are here now and I am not its lord."

'I answered him, "Give me half of your treasure. Then I will go away

'So, he took my hand and accompanied me to a large room. He touched one of the walls and it opened. Then we walked down a corridor. He said a magic word and a granite door opened. The Emperor covered his eyes with his hands to protect them from the light of the jewels there. It was really marvellous inside. There were huge tortoise-shells full of pearls, and many other wonderful jewels.

'Then the Emperor said to me, "This is my house of treasure, and half of it is yours. But you must go tonight. My father the Sun must not see this: I cannot kill a man in the city."

'I answered him, "The gold and all the precious jewels are yours. I only want your little ring."

'The Emperor frowned. "It is only a ring of lead," he cried, "and it has no value. Take your half of the treasure and go away from my city."

'"No," I answered, "I know that it is really the Ring of Riches." 'The Emperor trembled and said, "Take all the treasure and go from my city. You can also have my half of the treasure."

'Then I did something strange, but it is not important. What is important is that I put the Ring of Riches in a cave. You can arrive there in one day. The owner of this Ring is richer than all the kings of the world.'

But the young fisherman laughed. 'Love is better than riches,' he cried, 'and the little mermaid loves me.'

'No, nothing is better than riches,' said the soul.

'Love is better,' answered the young fisherman. He went back to the sea, and the soul walked away and cried.

CHAPTER SIX
The Souls of Third Journey

After the third year, the soul came down to the sea and called the young fisherman. He came out of the sea and said, 'Why do you call me?'

The soul answered, 'Come nearer. I want to speak to you because I saw marvellous things.'

So he came nearer, and sat in the water and listened.

The soul said to him, 'I went to an inn near a river in a city. I sat with sailors and they ordered food and drink. After some time an old man entered with a carpet and a lute. He put the carpet on the floor. When he played the lute, a girl came in and began to dance. There was a veil on her face, and she had no shoes. Her feet moved on the carpet like little white pigeons. It was really marvellous and it is only one day away from here.'

The young fisherman heard these words. He remembered that the little mermaid had no feet and could not dance. He thought, 'It is only one day away, and I can return to my love.' He laughed, stood up in the water and walked towards the beach.

When he reached the beach, his soul ran towards him and entered him. Then the young fisherman saw on the sand the shadow of the body, the body of the soul.

They began their journey, and the next evening they came to a city.

The young fisherman said to his soul, 'Does she dance in this city?'

His soul answered him, 'Not in this city, but another. Let's enter this city anyway.'

So they entered and walked in the streets. The young fisherman saw a silver cup on a stall in the Street of the Jewellers. His soul said to him, 'Take that silver cup and hide it.'

So he took the silver cup and hid it, and they went quickly out of the city.

When they were far from the city, the young fisherman threw the cup away. He said to his soul,

'It was not a good thing to take the cup and hide it!'

But his soul answered him, 'Calm down, calm down.'

On the evening of the second day they came to a city. The young fisherman said to his soul, 'Does she dance in this city?'

His soul answered him, 'Not in this city, but in another. Let's enter this city anyway.'

So they entered and walked in the streets. In the Street of the Sellers of Sandals, the young fisherman saw a child. His soul said to him, 'Hit that child!' So he hit the child, and the child cried, and then they went quickly out of the city.

When they were far from the city, the young fisherman became angry and said to his soul, 'It was not a good thing to hit the child!'

But his soul answered him, 'Calm down, calm down.'

On the evening of the third day they came to a city. The young fisherman said to his soul, 'Does she dance in this city?'

His soul answered him, 'Perhaps this is the city. Let's enter.' They walked in the streets, but the young fisherman could not find the inn near the river. He wanted to leave, but his soul said to him, 'Let's stay here tonight. Perhaps there are robbers outside.'

So the fisherman sat down in the marketplace. After some time a merchant came and said to him, 'Why are you here? The market is closed.'

The young fisherman answered him, 'I can't find an inn in this city. I have no family here and I need a room for the night.'

'We are all of the same family,' said the merchant, 'and one God made us. Come with me. I have a room.'

The young fisherman followed the merchant to his house. The merchant gave him good food and a comfortable room. The young fisherman then went to sleep. After three hours his soul woke him and said, 'Go to the room of the merchant and kill him, and take his gold.'

The young fisherman went into the merchant's room. There was a sword near his feet, and nine purses of gold next to the bed. When he touched the sword, the merchant woke up and said, 'Why do you want to kill me? I gave you good food and a room. I was kind to you!'

His soul said to the young fisherman, 'Hit him!' So he hit him and the merchant lost consciousness. He then took the nine purses of gold, and went quickly away from the city.

When they were far from the city, the young fisherman said to his soul, 'It was bad to hit the merchant and take his gold!'

But his soul answered him, 'Calm down, calm down.'

'No,' cried the young fisherman, 'I cannot be calm. You told me to do bad things and I hate these things. I also hate you. Why did you do these things?'

His soul answered him, 'When you sent me out into the world, you did not give me a heart. So I learned to do all these things and love them.'

'What are you saying?' murmured the young fisherman.

'You know,' answered his soul. 'You did not give me a heart. So stay calm. You will give other people all kinds of pain, and you will receive all kinds of pleasure.'

The young fisherman said to his soul, 'No, you are bad, and I forgot about my love and did many bad things because of you.'

His soul answered him, 'You did not forget that you sent me away without a heart. Let's go to another city and enjoy life together. We have nine purses of gold.'

But the young fisherman took the nine purses of gold, and threw them on the ground.

'No, I will not come with you, and I will send you away again,' said the young fisherman.

He turned his back to the moon. With the little knife he tried to cut his shadow from his feet to eliminate his soul. But his soul did not leave him, and said to him, 'The magic of the witch will not work. It only works once in a man's life. I will stay with you forever, and this is your punishment and your recompense.'

Now the young fisherman was desperate and cried because his soul was very bad. When it was day the young fisherman said to his soul, 'I will tie my hands together. Then I cannot do what you tell me to do. 1 will return to the bay because my love sings there. I will call her. I will tell her about the bad things I did and the bad things you did to me.'

When he arrived on the beach, he freed his hands and called the mermaid. But she did not come.

His soul laughed at him and said, 'Your love gives you little joy. Come with me to the Valley of Pleasure. That is better for you.'

The young fisherman did not answer his soul. He built a house by the bay and lived there for a year. Every morning he called the mermaid, and every midday he called her again, and at night he spoke her name. But she never came to see him, and he did not see her anywhere.

His soul always asked him to do bad things. But the young fisherman never listened to him because the power of his love was so great.

CHAPTER SEVEN

Love

After another year, the soul thought, 'I tempted him with bad, and his love is stronger than I am. I will now tempt him with good, and perhaps he will come with me.'

So he spoke to the young fisherman and said, 'I told you about the joy of the world, and you did not listen to me. Now I will tell you about the pain in the world, and maybe you will listen. Pain is the Lord of this world, and nobody can escape it. Some people do not have clothes and other people do not have food, and others are ill. Come, let's go and help these people.

Why do you wait here for your love?

What is love? Why do you think it is so important?'

But the young fisherman did not answer. The power of his love was so great. Every morning he called the mermaid, and every midday he called her again, and at night he spoke her name. But she never came to see him, and he did not see her anywhere.

After the second year, the soul said to the fisherman, 'I tempted you with bad, and I tempted you with good, and your love is stronger than I am. So, I will not tempt you anymore, but can I please enter your heart and be there with you again?'

'Of course you can enter,' said the young fisherman. 'I am sure you suffered when you did not have a heart.'

'But I can find no place to enter because there is love all around your heart. There's no space for me,' cried the soul.

'I am very sorry,' said the young fisherman.

Just then he heard a terrible cry of sadness from the sea. The young fisherman ran to the beach. The black waves came quickly to the beach. They carried something that was whiter than silver. There at his feet the young fisherman saw the dead body of the little mermaid.

He sat down next to her, and he kissed her cold red mouth. He told the dead mermaid about his soul and all the bad things. He put her little hands around his neck, and he touched her neck with his fingers. His joy was bitter, and his pain was full of strange happiness.

The black sea came nearer and nearer to them.

'Run away,' said his soul. 'The sea is coming closer and closer. Go away! It will kill you. Run away to a safe place. But please do not send me into another world without a heart.'

But the young fisherman did not listen to his soul. He said to the little mermaid, 'Love is better than wisdom, and more precious than riches, and more beautiful than the feet of the daughters of men. I called you in the morning, but you did not come. The moon heard your name, but you did not listen to me. I was bad when I abandoned you. But your love was always with me, and it was always stronger than bad and good. And now that you are dead, I will die with you also.'

His soul implored him to leave. But his love was too great and he did not listen to his soul. The sea came near and tried to cover him with its waves.

When he knew that the end was near, the young fisherman kissed the cold lips of the mermaid, and his heart broke. It broke because it was so full of love. Then the soul finally entered his heart, and the sea covered the young fisherman with its waves the Fullers.

CHAPTER EIGHT
The Field of the Fullers

In the morning the priest said, 'I will go and bless the sea because it was not calm last night.' Monks, musicians and many other people went with him.

When the priest reached the beach he saw the young fisherman. He was dead in the water and the body of the little mermaid was in his arms. The priest frowned and said, 'I will not bless the sea or anything in the sea. The young fisherman abandoned God for love, and the punishment of God killed him and his love. Now take his body and the body of the mermaid and bury them in the corner of the Field of the Fullers. Do not put any sign there.'

The people put the dead bodies in a deep hole in the corner of the Field of the Fullers. They covered the hole with earth. No sweet herbs grew there.

Three years later on a holy day, the priest went to the chapel to speak to the people about the anger of God.

When he went to the altar, he saw that there were strange flowers on the altar. Their strange beauty worried him and their perfume was sweet. He was particularly happy and he did not understand why he was so happy.

He wanted to speak to them about the anger of God. But the beauty of the white flowers worried him, and their perfume was sweet. He did not speak of the anger of God. He spoke of the love of God. And he did not know why he spoke like this.

When he finished speaking, the people cried, and his eyes were full of tears. He was in a dream, and he said to his deacons, 'What are the flowers on the altar? Where do they come from?'

They answered him, 'We do not know what kind of flowers they are, but they come from the corner of the Field of the Fullers.' The priest trembled, and returned to his house and prayed.

Early the next morning he left his house with monks, musicians and many other people. He walked to the beach and blessed the sea, and all the wild things in it.

He also blessed the fauns, and the little things that dance in the forest. He blessed all things in the world of God, and the people were full of joy. But the people of the sea went to another part of the sea, and they never came back again.